Peter Riley

The Highways and Byways of Jack the Ripper

Poplar Workhouse

P & D Riley

First published 2001 by

P & D Riley
12 Bridgeway East,
Cheshire WA7 6LD
England,
e-mail: pdriley@lineone.net

Copyright © 2001 by Peter Riley
ISBN: 1 874712 49 2

British Library Cataloguing in Publication Data
A catalogue Record for this book is available from the British Library

Printed in England by Walter Brown Printers, 92 Newton Road, Lowton, Warrington, WA3 1DG.

Introduction

SOMEWHERE, in a cold, damp grave, at this very moment in time lies the remains of an ordinary man. Ordinary, that is, in the sense that he gave no indication to those who knew him in life as being the world's most talked about criminal. His family were unaware; his doctor, landlord, friends, colleagues, acquaintances, neighbours, and, finally, the undertakers who committed his body to the grave, were all unaware that this ordinary man - this (perhaps) cheerful father; this (perhaps) satisfactory lover; this (perhaps) pleasant friend and neighbour - was in fact the infamous, vicious criminal known in the annals of crime as Jack the Ripper!

Over the past century or so, the name Jack the Ripper has become a household word for evil. It has also become a nickname which flows easily off the tongue when modern day mass murderers are compared with the Victorian reprobate. The vision, helped through the media of film and television, is of a dark figure clutching a large knife and Gladstone bag as he disappears into the fog of Victorian Whitechapel in London's East End.

And there, for most people, the vision ends. There is nothing enticing beyond the uncanny choice of name, which has undoubtedly secured the anonymous killer his position as number one in the hierarchy of killers. Jack the Ripper as a tradename could not have been a better choice if he had employed an advertising agency to choose one for him. But what of the fiend behind the mask of obscurity? What of the man himself? Was he, indeed, the good father and lover? Was he the good worker who was the envy of his friends, and the pride of his employer? Questions which are obviously impossible to answer but they are asked to remind us that this killer did exist in a normal day to day role, albeit in a disturbed manner on occasions which saw him slaughter his helpless victims.

He did not go around town wearing a sign saying "I am Jack the Ripper." On the contrary, he probably voiced, along with the rest of the population of London, his disgust at the killings to those who would listen. Indeed, if we had the power to know, this anonymous man may well have been at the centre of a group of local residents forming a vigilante group in Whitechapel. Of course this is all pure speculation, but the fact remains that, as you read this, somewhere in a quiet corner of a graveyard lies the bones of Jack the Ripper, and his name (his real one of course) is no doubt filed in the deaths section of the British Public Records Office. Oh that we had the power to know which file to open!

Jack the Ripper is a subject which constantly intrigues readers throughout the world and the sites of Whitechapel and Spitalfields play a major part in presenting the atmosphere of the ripper saga, despite the fact that none of the sites of the killings remain in their original state. Having said that, however, for the most part the streets themselves remain, streets which Jack and his unfortunate victims trod in the 1880s; and even today, well over a century later, visitors seeking out Jack the Ripper can thrill to the chase as they tread the highways and byways of the districts of the East End.

This little book, which is not meant to add anything new to the story of who Jack the Ripper was (there are enough such books already!), is meant instead to give a feel of the atmosphere of Whitechapel, Spitalfields, and parts of London as it was in the Ripper's day, and as it is today. Some of the pictures, by necessity, have been seen before, but many of them are presented here for the first time.

I would like to hear from readers who own other pictures or photographs of Whitechapel and Spitalfields which have not appeared in print before as it may be possible to offer the chance for them to appear in any future edition of this book. Please write to me at the address on page 2, or e-mail me, and all letters will be acknowledged.

Peter Riley

Acknowledgments

The publishers would like to thank the following for their help in making this publication possible:

Robin Odell, Ross Strachan, Paul Begg,
The Public Records Office, Tower Hamlets Library,
New Scotland Yard, Euston Films.

Dedicated to 'Ripperologists' everywhere, especially those who are unable to pay a personal visit to the streets of Whitechapel and Spitalfields in their never ending quest!

Jack the Ripper
An outline of the murders

IN George Yard Buildings in the slums of Spitalfields, East London, the death of Martha Turner, or Tabram, aged 35, on August 7, 1888, provoked little interest despite the fact that she had been stabbed 39 times in the chest, throat and abdomen. Indeed, so little interest was taken in Turner's murder, that a report did not even appear in the press until three days later as the inquest into her death opened.

There would, without doubt, have been a far wider interest if the police, press and public had only known then that Turner, a prostitute, or 'unfortunate' as the Victorians called them, was believed to have been the first victim of a mad man soon to become known throughout the world as Jack the Ripper.

MARTHA TURNER
(or Tabram)

Aged 35, married, but living apart from husband. Mother of three children, was an 'unfortunate' (prostitute) who frequented Whitechapel and area close to London docks. Lived at 4 Star Place, Commercial Road, and was unknown to residents of George Yard Buildings where her body was found at approximately 5am by resident John Reeves who was leaving home to look for work in nearby markets. Another resident, Albert Crow, told police he had seen a huddled figure on the landing at 3.30am but took no notice. Was this the already murdered body of Turner?

But Turner was an overweight, unattractive woman, the like of which were so common around Spitalfields and neighbouring Whitechapel as to provoke no comment, no outcry. Indeed, 1888 was a very bad year for murder, and scarcely a day seemed to go by without some corpse being discovered in the gutter, or in one of the thousands of back alleyways of that city within a city.

Gunthorpe St, (George Yard) as it looks today

Above: George Yard Buildings as they looked at the time of Jack the Ripper and, right, the same site as it looks today.

DURWARD STREET
Formerly
BUCK'S ROW

Only 300 yards from George Yard stood Buck's Row, now Durward Street, where on this spot (now demolished) was murdered Mary Ann Nichols, also known as 'Polly'. The streets was like thousands of others at the time, long, narrow and very dark, and this gateway provided perfect cover in its time, offering the ideal spot for Jack the Ripper to entice his victim into deep shadow where he committed his appalling crime. Many ripper followers claim this murder, and not that of Martha Turner, was the first in the Ripper's catalogue of crime.

THREE weeks later, in Buck's Row (now Durward Street), Whitechapel, and only a few hundred yards from where Turner was killed, another unfortunate was savagely murdered. The victim was Mary Ann Nichols, aged 42, a married woman who was separated from her husband. She had suffered terrible injuries. her throat had been cut, and she had been mutilated, although this was not discovered until she had been removed to a nearby workhouse mortuary where she had been stripped by a workhouse pauper in readiness for an autopsy.

Durward Street (Buck's Row) as it looks today. The site of Nichols' killing was at the bottom right of the picture

The police could do nothing. The killer was unknown and had left no obvious clues, for, of course, this was long before the forensic science skills known to crime fighters today. For all intents and purposes, the assassin had disappeared like a ghost. He had worked swiftly and silently, for some residents of Essex Wharf, Bucks Row, directly opposite the murder scene, admitted to being awake at the estimated time of the murder, between 3.15am and 3.45am, on August 31, 1888, told police they had heard no sound from the cobbled street.

MARY ANN NICHOLS
(known as 'Polly')

Aged 42. Married but living apart from her husband William. Mother of 5 children, she was also an 'unfortunate' with no fixed abode, and frequented several local 'doss' houses in Whitechapel and Spitalfields. Her body was found in Buck's Row at approximately 3.45am by Charles reports Cross and Robert reports say John) Paul while on their way to work. An hour or so before her death she had been turned away from 18 Thrawl Street because she was the worse for drink and did not have money for a bed. It's claimed she said as she left: "Never mind, I'll soon get my doss money, see what a jolly bonnet I've got now!" Her bonnet went missing and was never seen again. Was the bonnet kept as a grisly souvenir by Jack the Ripper?

Buck's Row as it looked in the 1970s

A BODY ON THE PAVEMENT.

Top Left: Essex Wharf, Durward Street, as it looks today. Top Right: The 'Roebuck' pub which stood on the corner of Buck's Row and Brady Street. Below Left: Discovering Nichols' body. Bottom Right: The scene of the killing today.

With the killing of Mary Nichols, the East End began to take notice, and considerable space was given in the press about the murder, but police still had no clues. While London was still talking about the murder of Nichols, the killer shook the capital to its very foundations only a week later. It was September 8, 1888, when yet another murdered woman was found in the rear yard of 29 Hanbury Street, off Commercial Street, Spitalfields, only 10 minutes walk from Buck's Row and less than a five minutes walk away from George Yard Buildings.

Victim number three was identified as Annie Chapman, 47, a widow. She, like her fellow victims, was a prostitute, and was nicknamed 'Dark Annie' because of her habit of keeping her opinions to herself most of the time. Chapman's body was found by John Davis, a market porter, who lived at 29 Hanbury Street with several other families. He later told police he had risen from bed at about 5.45am, and after making a drink had gone into the backyard where he found the body. She had been viciously disembowelled after having her throat cut.

Davis had ran to Commercial Street Police Station, about 200 yards away, and within a few minutes, for such was the nature of the East End, the streets were full of policemen and curiosity seekers. Indeed so enterprising were some neighbours that they allowed the curious to peep onto the scene from their back windows for a one penny fee, and business was

HANBURY STREET

Hanbury Street ran from Commercial Street in the heart of Spitalfields to Brick Lane and beyond to Bakers Row, close to Buck's Row, and in the backyard of 29 Hanbury Street, (centre of pic) Jack the Ripper slaughtered Annie Chapman, also known as 'Dark Annie'. The front of the building was used as a cat's meat business and its upstairs rooms had several lodgers, none of whom heard anything to disturb their sleep. The shop later became a barber's and was still occupied until the late 1960's when it was demolished with the rest of the row of squalid properties. The site was later built upon by a local brewery and the only site of 29 Hanbury Street today is a brick wall, though properties opposite remind us of how the street once looked.

Above: Hanbury Street as it looks today. The site of 29 Hanbury Street was located on the left side of the street, approximately where the second tree is now growing. This was once a bustling street filled with thousands of people who lived and worked in the maze of alleyways and courtyard which filtered off it, but the street now far quieter than it used to be and trade, for the most part, has gone elsewhere.

brisk all day on September 8, and for several days afterwards when there was nothing to see but the back yard.

In the yard police found a wet leather apron and a small envelope flap which bore the name Sussex Regiment, and they took these items to be clues. It was an unfortunate decision so far as one man was concerned, a Polish shoe repairer named John Pizer, for he always wore a leather apron for his craft, and in no time the almost frenzied citizens of Whitechapel were accusing him of the murder, and he was taken into police custody at one point for his own safety.

It is true that Pizer was known locally as Leather Apron, but he successfully cleared himself of having any connection with the case, but only after he had locked himself in his home in Mulberry Street, Whitechapel, for three days with his family. He later emerged from the inquest into Chapman's death and successfully took out libel suits against a number of newspapers who had foolishly claimed he was the Whitechapel killer.

All this friction and embarrassment need not have happened in the first place, for at the inquest, the leather apron found in the yard was identified as the property of John Richardson, whose mother owned 29 Hanbury Street. He told the inquest that the apron had been left in the yard for several days after he had washed it under a tap.

ANNIE CHAPMAN
(known as 'Dark Annie')

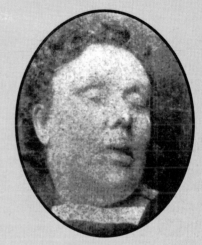

Aged 47. A widow who often slept at a 'doss house' at 35 Dorset Street, opposite Spitalfields Church. She was the mother of three children, two girls and a boy, though one daughter died in 1882. Whether this death started her on the road to ruin is not known, but shortly afterwards she abandoned her family and moved to London. Her husband John died in 1886, and nothing is known of the whereabouts of her two surviving children. She variously hawked goods but also turned to prostitution when necessary to make ends meet. Normally lived in Crossingham's lodging house at 35 Dorset Street, close to where Mary Jane Kelly was later killed by Jack the Ripper.

Entry to the rear of 29 Hanbury Street was via a passageway which led past stairs to upper floors and out into the back yard where Chapman's mutilated remains were found.

The body was found lying at the foot of two steps leading into the yard, almost touching the wooden fence separating 29 from its neighbour.

Hanbury Street is one of the oldest streets in the Spitalfields area and was originally called Brown's Lane. The street was given its present name after Sampson Hanbury, a Quaker who had joined the board of local brewer's Truman's, and it is with a touch of irony that the site of number 29 Hanbury Street should eventually be incorporated into the brewery site.

The backyard of 29 Hanbury St

Doorway to 29 Hanbury St. Jack the Ripper took Chapman through the doorway on the left leading to the back yard where she was found.

The police were getting nowhere. Their 'clues' had been useless, and their efforts to track down the elusive killer had proved just as hopeless. Not that efforts were spared, for they questioned all the residents in the hundreds of common lodging houses in Whitechapel and Spitalfields, and they arrested people on the least suspicion. But it was not enough, and before long the press and citizens of London were demanding that heads roll. Questions were asked in the Houses of

Hanbury Street, Spitalfields, pictured in 1938 by William Stewart, author of '*Jack the Ripper A New Theory*'. It is interesting to compare this picture with the photograph on page 12 which was taken from the same spot.

Commercial Street, Spitalfields, pictured in 1907, which is a fascinating picture to Ripperologists, for it shows the *Ten Bells* public house on the right, which was used by all the victims of Jack the Ripper, and which still stands, and the *Britannia* public house on the left, which stood on the corner of Dorset Street, and only yards from where Mary Jane Kelly was slaughtered by the killer.

The *Ten Bells* public house as it looks today

Parliament, and open hostility blew up between Sir Charles Warren, the Metropolitan Police Commissioner, and Henry Matthews, the Home Secretary.

While all this activity was going on, a letter arrived on September 27, 1888, at the office of the Central News agency in London, in which the author cynically abused the police and talked of continuing his work by clipping the ears off his next victim. The letter was signed **Jack the Ripper**, the first time the name had ever been used.

Three days later, on September 30, the world at large, and London in particular, were to be totally shocked by the audacity of the Ripper, who until that time had been known simply as 'The Whitechapel Killer.' For on that date he slit the throat of Elizabeth 'Long Liz' Stride, a Swedish

HENRIQUES STREET
Formerly
Berner Street

THIS little street runs from the now very busy Whitechapel Road, and once was a street of squalid houses, beerhouses and corner shops. The street today has changed beyond recognition from the days of Jack the Ripper, and almost all the properties have disappeared. On the site of Dutfield's Yard, where Elizabeth Stride was killed, now stands Harry Gosling Primary School, which was built in the 1920s after the east side of the street was redeveloped.

This was one of many rough streets in the neighbourhood, and it is surprising that Jack escaped with so many people moving about the street or standing at their front doors well after midnight. The street name was changed after the murder.

woman who had lived in London for some years, and it is believed that he only failed to carry out his 'trademark' of mutilating the body because of the arrival of a hawker named Louis Diemshutz, who turned his horse and cart into Dutfield's Yard at the side of 40 Berner Street (now Henriques Street), Whitechapel, about a mile from the previous murders.

The horse shied and refused to enter the pitch dark courtyard, and it was this that caused Diemshutz to investigate and subsequently discover the recently killed body of Elizabeth Stride, who, it was said, could only speak in broken English. Experts have theorised that Jack the Ripper was still in the yard at the time, and after Diemshutz had run for help into the Working Men's Club which had its entrance in the yard, the killer had escaped into Berner Street.

Within minutes Berner Street was swarming with people, despite the fact that it was 1am. And while their anger was brewing Jack the Ripper struck again only 40 minutes later in Mitre Square, which is situated within the boundary of the City of London, a different police jurisdiction to the previous murders which had occurred with the Metropolitan Police area served from Scotland Yard.

The Mitre Square victim was named as Catherine Eddowes, and her mutilations were far worse than anything seen so far. It appears that Jack had become so frustrated at having been disturbed with Elizabeth Stride that he had then released his anger and

Finding Elizabeth Stride's body

ELIZABETH STRIDE
(known as 'Long Liz')

frustration on Eddowes. He had worked extremely fast, and with some skill, for Mitre Square was patrolled every 15 minutes, and at 1.30am there was no sign of a body, according to the beat policeman, PC Edward Watkins, but at 1.45am he discovered Eddowes' body. It was found that the killer, in addition to horrific mutilation of the body, had sliced her face, including her ears. The letter prophesy, it appeared, had come true.

London was in a panic. Queen Victoria was demanding answers, and a row was developing between Metropolitan Police Commissioner Warren and Acting City of London Police Commissioner, Major Henry Smith. Smith was, by all accounts, a good policeman, a true professional and a total contrast to the 'Major Blimp' image presented by his counterpart whose major role in life prior to joining Scotland Yard was as a colonial

Aged 45, Elizabeth Stride was born in Torslanda, Sweden, in 1843, as Elizabeth Gustafsdotter. When she was 22 she gave birth to a still-born girl and gave her occupation even then as a prostitute. She moved to Britain in 1866 and three years later married John Stride at St Giles in the Fields Church in London. She gave her address at the time of her marriage as 67 Gower Street. Later claimed that her husband and children had drowned on the steamer *Princess Alice* which sank in the Thames at Woolwich, but according to authors Paul Begg, Keith Skinner and Martin Fido, writing in their *Jack the Ripper A-Z*, John Stride died in 1884 in Bromley. She later variously lived in lodging houses in Flower and Dean Street and Dorset Street.

MITRE SQUARE

Scene of the murder in the 1970s

ONCE tucked away in a very quiet backwater of the City of London, but only a few yards away from the boundary with Whitechapel, Mitre Square is now totally changed from the days of Jack the Ripper, but the changes came slowly. In fact it is only since the 1980s that the Victorian buildings, particularly the well known Kearley and Tonge's warehouse, in which watchman George Morris helped PC Edward Watkins after the policeman had found Catherine Eddowes' body in the darkest corner of the square, were demolished.

Today the square is far more open than it was, though even now there is still a degree of solitude in the square at certain times of the day and night, and it is regularly frequented by Jack the Ripper hunters!

soldier. Smith's men were soon on the trail of Jack the Ripper, but an important clue found in a doorway in Goulston Street, Whitechapel, was over the police boundary in Whitechapel, and Warren ordered it wiped out. This was a sample of handwriting in chalk written on a wall, within a couple of feet of where pursuing City men had found a piece of apron which had evidently been used by Jack to wipe his hands. The piece of apron had allegedly been cut from an apron worn by Eddowes.

Scene of the murder as it looks today

Despite continuing police pressure, including a farcical attempt by Warren to bring in bloodhounds to search a well trodden metropolitan district (the dogs actually got lost on a training exercise!), the killer remained at large.

Five weeks passed before Saucy Jack struck again. This time the victim was Mary Jane Kelly, aged 25, the youngest and prettiest of the victims, who also used the name Marie Jeanette evidently in an attempt to convince her 'clients' that she was in a class of prostitutes higher than the hundreds which then plied their trade in Whitechapel and Spitalfields.

Kelly was found at about 11am on the morning of November 9, 1888, completely mutilated inside her tiny hovel, a room in Miller's Court, Dorset Street, (later renamed Duval Street), Spitalfields. She was so badly cut up that it took surgeons more than six hours to piece her together for purposes of identification.

There were no real clues except for some burnt clothing in the fire grate, and a kettle whose spout had melted in intense heat. In the mind of some Ripperologists it gave way to suggestions that Jack the Ripper might have escaped the scene dressed as a woman.

But for all the speculation, all the police activity, Jack the Ripper was never captured. Sir Charles Warren resigned on the day Kelly was discovered and disappeared for ever, except in the imagination of

CATHERINE EDDOWES

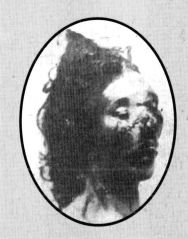

Aged 46, Catherine (or Catharine according to some accounts) Eddowes was born in Wolverhampton in the Midlands. Her mother died when she was 13 and she is believed to have moved in with her aunt while her brothers and sisters were sent to the Workhouse in Bermondsey, London.

Although known to like a few drinks, she is said to have been a cheerful character who earned most of her lodging money by selling items on the streets or by scrounging wherever she could. She had three children, two sons and a daughter, by Thomas Conway whom she claimed to have married, but no marriage record has been found. The marriage failed through her drinking habits and she entered the inevitable life of living in doss houses.

Above: Mitre Square shown in all its Victorian gloom and the ideal spot for the work of Jack the Ripper.

countless writers and criminologists who still hope they can solve this greatest of mysteries and at last identify for certain the spectre of Jack the Ripper.

MARY JANE KELLY
(Also known as Marie Jeanette)

NOT much is known about the early life of Mary Jane Kelly, the alleged final victim of Jack the Ripper, who, at 25 years old, was the youngest and the prettiest of his victims - and certainly the most abused by his knife! According to what information she gave to her friends and drinking cronies in Miller's Court and The Ten Bells, she was born in Ireland and moved to Wales as a child with her brothers and sister. In 1879 she married a man named Davies, but he died in a pit explosion in 1882. Mary Jane then went to live with a cousin before moving to London in 1884 and worked in a West End brothel. Drinking was probably responsible for her further downfall, and she eventually ended up in various lodgings in Thrawl Street, Brick Lane and Flower and Dean Street before her ill-fated move to Dorset St where she died.

For several years the *Ten Bells* pub in Spitalfields changed its name to the more notorious *Jack the Ripper*, and its front window listed the series of killings, but objections from pressure groups caused the brewery to return the pub to its original name

Left: A typical East End street pictured about 1900, while pictured right is a Whitechapel 'doss house' which were so common across the district until well into the 20th century.

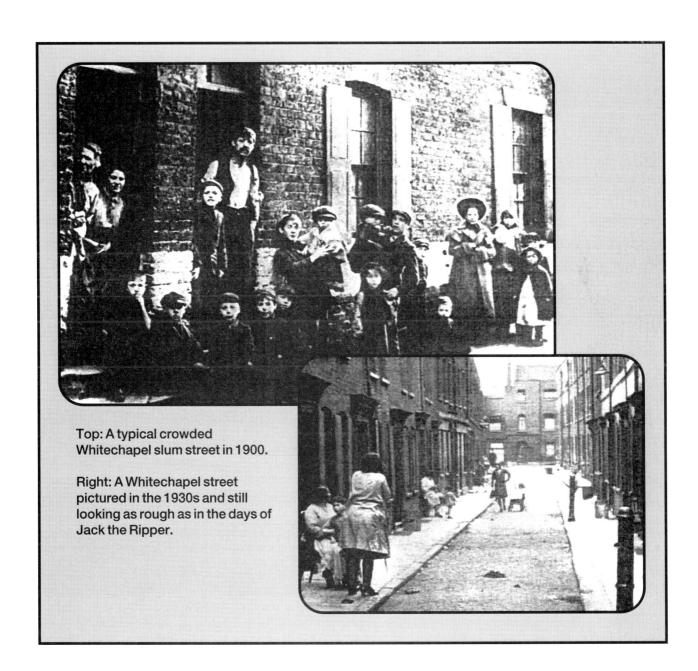

Top: A typical crowded Whitechapel slum street in 1900.

Right: A Whitechapel street pictured in the 1930s and still looking as rough as in the days of Jack the Ripper.

Berner Street (now Henriques Street), Whitechapel, in the days of Jack the Ripper. The first victim of the 'Double Event' Elizabeth 'Long Liz' Stride was found lying dead with her throat cut against the wall of the International Working Men's Club through the double gates in the centre of the picture. It has been assumed by Ripper experts that the killer probably cut through the back streets, past the corner shop in the photograph, and wended his way to Mitre Square where he committed his second murder of the night.

An interesting comparison and a good demonstration of how much has changed in Whitechapel in the century since Jack the Ripper stalked these streets is this photograph of Berner Street (Henriques Street) as it looks today from the same spot as the picture on page 26. The properties have all long gone, and the scene of Elizabeth Stride's murder is now incorporated into the grounds of this primary school.

Three views of Flower and Dean Street. Above left as it looked in the 1930s, and (right) as it looked in the 1970s following demolition of most of the properties.

Above left: Once called Flower and Dean Street, the very heart of Jack the Ripper territory, this street is now called Lolesworth Close and has been totally redeveloped since the late 1970s.

Above right: Pictured in 1978, when all that remained was a corner pub, is Thrawl Street, Spitalfields, where, at number 18, Mary Ann Nichols lodged. It was after being turned away on August 31, 1888, that she walked to her death in Buck's Row

Above: Fournier Street, opposite Spitalfields Church, was home to Huguenot silk spinners and the haunt of local prostitutes. This modern picture shows it hasn't changed much in the past 100 years. Top Right: Vagrants in 'Itchy Park', outside the church in 1900. Bottom Right: The Casual Ward of Whitechapel Workhouse about 1910

The changing face of Whitechapel and Spitalfields is clearly shown in these pictures of the highways and byways of the district taken in the late 1970s when the district, much to the chagrin of Ripper enthusiasts, was being torn down. Above Left: Old Montague Street, where it was claimed Mary Ann Nichols' and Annie Chapman's bodies were taken to the mortuary. Left: Winthrop Street which ran parallel to Buck's Row, but which is now no longer a through road as it is incorporated into a new building project. Above Another shot of Winthrop Street looking in the opposite direction.

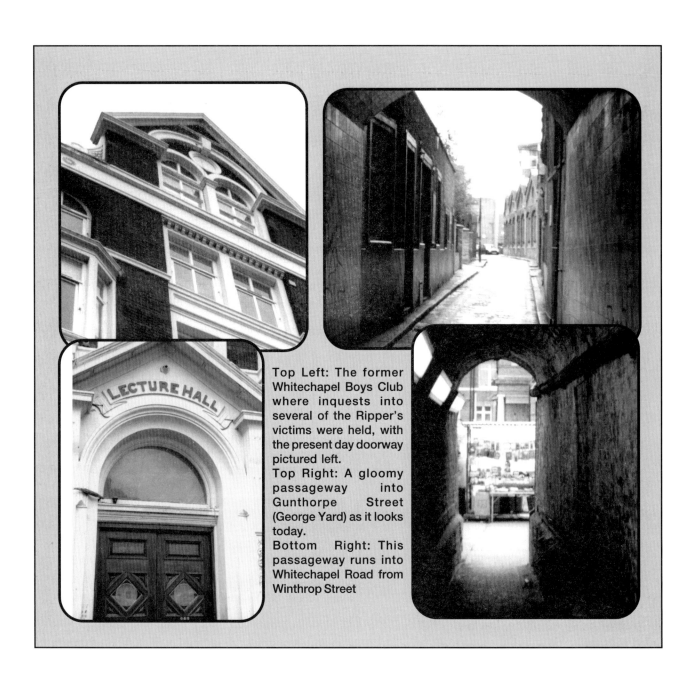

Top Left: The former Whitechapel Boys Club where inquests into several of the Ripper's victims were held, with the present day doorway pictured left.

Top Right: A gloomy passageway into Gunthorpe Street (George Yard) as it looks today.

Bottom Right: This passageway runs into Whitechapel Road from Winthrop Street

Four pictures of Spitalfields famous market all taken in different decades. Top left the 1970s; top right and bottom left, 2001, bottom right the 1930s

Homelessness has long been a major problem in Whitechapel, and finding a 'doss' for the night rings regularly throughout the Ripper saga, and these historic pictures show the problem all too clearly.

Top: Lining up to find a place in the Salvation Army hostel in the early 20th century.

Bottom: Inside the Salvation Army courtyard waiting for paperwork for food and lodgings.

Another varied diet of the way things have changed in Whitechapel is shown by these photographs.

Top: Waiting for admission to Whitechapel Workhouse, also known as 'The Spike' about 1900.

Right: Pictured in 2001 is the former Board School, now apartments, at the junction of Buck's Row, only yards from where Mary Ann Nichols was killed.

Top Right: The former Jack the Ripper pub sign at the now renamed Ten Bells.

Top: The Ten Bells Public house on the corner of Commercial Street and Fournier Street pictured in 1977 when it had changed its name to the more dramatic 'Jack the Ripper'.

Right: This modern photograph shows the former home of silk designer Anna Maria Garthwaite (1690-1763) at the corner of Wilkes Street and Frances Street, and still standing only yards from 29 Hanbury Street. It is a good example of houses in the area at the time the area was home to London's silk weavers.

White's Row,(top) showing the modern car park which now stands on the site of Dorset Street (above) from which Miller's Court, (right) scene of the murder of Mary Jane Kelly, the youngest and, some say, final victim of Jack the Ripper, was entered.

These two photographs taken in 2001 show the totally changed face of Mitre Square. On the left is a modern office block which now stands on the site of the famous Kearley and Tonge warehouse. On the right is 'Ripper's Corner' as it now looks. Incidentally, Ripper enthusiasts will be interested to know that the man sitting facing the camera is French composer Eric Sitbon, whose show 'Jack the Musical' is currently doing the European circuit, while the woman in the light clothing is singer Lisa Marshall who plays Annie Chapman in the production. They were coincidentally paying a 'courtesy' trip to the Ripper sites when this photograph was taken.

The sketch at the top of the page shows the spot where Catherine Eddowes was found as depicted in a contemporary newspaper of the time.

Mitre Street as it looks today. The entrance to Mitre Square is on the right.

Two era's: The picture on the left shows Whitechapel High Street in the 1890s, while the picture on the right shows the corner of Henriques Street (Berner Street) and Commercial Road as it looks today.